Dead Man's Hand

ALSO BY JEFF WEDDLE

A Puncher's Chance (Rust Belt Press, 2019)

Citizen Relent (Unlikely Books, 2019)

It's Colder than Hell / Starving Elves Eat Reindeer Meat / Santa Claus is Dead (Alien Buddha Press, 2018)

Heart of the Broken World (Nixes Mate Books, 2017)

Comes to This (Nixes Mate Books, 2017)

When Giraffes Flew (Southern Yellow Pine, 2015)

Librarian's Guide to Negotiation: Winning Strategies for the Digital Age (co-author, Information Today 2012)

Betray the Invisible (OEOCO, 2012)

Bohemian New Orleans: The Story of the Outsider and Loujon Press (University Press of Mississippi, 2007)

Dead Man's Hand

poems by
Jeff Weddle

Poetic Justice Books
Port St. Lucie, Florida

©2019 Jeff Weddle

book design and layout: SpiNDec, Port Saint Lucie, FL
cover image: *Deal with It*, 2019, Kris Haggblom

All rights reserved.

No part of this book may be used or reproduced in any manner whatsoever without written permission except in the case of brief quotations embodied in critical articles and reviews. Members of educational institutions and organizations wishing to photocopy any of the work for classroom use, or authors, artists and publishers who would like to obtain permission for any material in the work, should contact the publisher.

Printed in the United States of America.
Published by Poetic Justice Books
Port Saint Lucie, Florida
www.poeticjusticebooks.com

ISBN: 978-1-950433-27-8

FIRST EDITION
10 9 8 7 6 5 4 3 2 1

Always for Jill

contents

Right Now	3
Enough	4
Expectations of Candles	5
Come Wish	6
Pear	7
The things we forget	8
The secret	9
Might as Well	10
Once Each Day	11
Lucy Love	12
Name in Lights	14
The Fight	15
Muse	17
Fireworks, Hampton Beach, NH	18
The Piano Spilled Waltzes	19
Always this Way	20
The Day Requires Sacrifice but I am Not Its Martyr	21
Unknown	22
Always for Jill	23
Once Upon	24
Gone Dancing	25
The Apartment	26
The Woman Poet	27
The Problem with Words	28
A Certain Day in August	29
Dancers	30
Jon and Gypsy	31
In This Life	33
But It's Okay	34

Like You, I Cannot Breathe	36
Drenched	37
Please Be Quiet	38
Sue Me	39
Trying To Tell You Something	40
Bouquet (*for Kate Bloom*)	41
Strange Actress	43
Portable Life	44
Failure to Communicate	45
Perspective	46
It's Simple	48
There was a Time	49
Just So	50
High Dive	51
The Cat	52
Chicken Fiasco	54
Bad Night on the Town	55
Hot Hot Hot	56
Six Pack	57
Pees	58
Some Kind of Patriotic Trip	59
You Know the Ones I Mean	60
It's Probably Just Me	61
The End of Things	62
How It Goes with Some	63

Lost	64
The Poets	65
When We Scream	66
Here is Truth for You	67
At the Feet of the Master	68
Motion Sickness	69
Explication	70
I Love My Readers	71
Original	72
Legacy	73
Wake the Fuck Up	74
Coming Soon	75
Meaningful Dialog	76
No Rest or Peace of Solitude	80
Try This	81
Pax Americana	82
Psychopathic White Cowards in Dumbass America Today	83
Bad Day	85
Get Your Peanuts	88
Dead Man's Hand	89
This is So	90

Dead Man's Hand

Right Now

coffee
couch
cat
snoring dog
the donuts eaten
my feet up
cool morning
the day in flow

Enough

this daisy
like any daisy
imperfect
but enough

this cat
like any cat
imperfect
but enough

this moment
like every moment
imperfect
but enough

Expectations of Candles

Exhausted
by outrage

can't breathe
like underwater

there were
dances once

sweet air
and expectations
of candles

sometimes
it's all that's left

a play of notes
and whispers
in the dark

Come Wish

angelic night
when you
become the name
and the name is radiant

when we can finally
tell our stories
of who we
might be

angel dove night
rain after years
of drought

all we need of time
is stories
where we are radiant
or could be

where we are angelic

Pear

The pear
was delicious
and sweet
wet upon
my face
succulent
a better
pear
than I
have ever
tasted

Thank you
for sharing
with me

I must
eat the rest
before
they get
too ripe

Though
I am sorry
you do not
like them

I am
grateful
for the gift

and will
repay you
with wet kisses

and dreams
of sweet delight

The things we forget

small daydreams
become a storyline
which writes itself

and some days
are like a circus
in blue cotton

and bring people
to your life
when you
are the stranger

bring them
for colorful reasons
that continue to matter
when they have
been forgotten

and clowns disown
their pratfalls
and twice-told
magic fails

The secret

There is one soul
and you and I and the cats
and every woman
man fish bug bird
and all other things
here and flung wide
across the void
everything
that lives now
or ever has or will
is that soul dancing
in a dream
or playing a game
or trying to awaken
and all is one and forever
and love is what happens
when the soul sees itself
hungry in the eyes of another

Might as Well

It might as well be love
but it is a cat instead
pretty much the same

sometimes it might as well be love
but it is a smile from a stranger
in the supermarket
buying the grapes
you did not even consider until now

it might as well be a lifetime of joy
but it is the sun going down in the west
beyond the fading hawks
and all the golden clouds

it might as well be sorrow
as the cat tires of your hand
and shifts to a more comfortable
aspect of her glory

it might as well be heaven
with God in tears on bended knee

it might as well be death
or the child inside your heart
running for its life
aglow with all the stars
and just as fleeting

Once Each Day

The ancient said:
"To be happy
allow yourself
to fall in love
once each day
as I am in love
with you, now."

She turned away
embarrassed.

Ages later
as became her habit
she could not
break her gaze
from the young
and handsome
nurse fussing
at her bedside.

He was a fresh dream
and tomorrow
was still alive
with chance.

Lucy Love

I.

I asked her if she didn't know better
than to take rides from strange men.
She asked me how strange I was
and gave me that look
the one I would come to know and fear.
Her name was Lucy
and I asked where she was heading.
"Just up the road," she told me at the fork.
"Whichever road you think might be the one."

II.

Lucy parked at the end of the trail.
It was just after three a.m.
She had been driving for hours
and was scared I was dead.
The baby's screams kept her company
in the constant rain.
I managed a low moan and moved my arm.
Lucy was too far gone to notice,
but we talked about all of it
the next day, after the burial.

III.

We were hungry after. Lucy.
It wouldn't be light for a couple of hours.
I couldn't stop crying.
I wanted you and I couldn't hide the tears.
Lucy. Ravenous, I say.
The dark is best for hiding,
but only deceives the wicked.
I would give a life for one more chance.
Lucy. Never satisfied.

IV.

How often they killed you
bare chested in empty houses
televisions thrown against walls
books unread and forgotten
always one more night to survive.
This will never end except with
tearful reunions in green fields.

Name in Lights

Theatrical on the small scale
like scrubbing bits of fat
from a silvery skillet

short fingernails
hardly up to the task

as the cat eats
what is left in her bowl
and the dog on the couch
dreams of rabbits or better

theatrical like the moon
dressed up for dancing

or your child
hiding in a bedroom

the stage set for screaming
and set for silence

theatrical to the heights
in this star turn
for no one special

bow down bow down
to empty seats

and a few blank faces

no curtain calls
no applause
no roses

The Fight

Half-past two in the morning
eating Dreamland
barbecue sauce
and white bread
at the kitchen table

Wondering who
would win
between Sonny Liston
and Mike Tyson
both in their prime
and raging

The Dreamland sauce
is so hot
I have to chase it
with banana yogurt
and my mouth
is still burning

Most people
would pick Tyson
because Liston fought
so long ago
and it's easy
to forget
how good he was

Iron Mike
was a beast
no doubt
but he won a lot of fights
because opponents
were terrified of him

Liston had the best jab
in the game
his arms were a mile long
and he didn't scare

It's a tough call
but the banana yogurt
is delicious
and I'm finally
feeling tired

I don't know anything
about anything

But it's time to try to sleep
and I'd take Liston in eight

Muse

When everyone
is sleeping
I sit in the dark
kitchen
and dream
idle dreams.

You don't know it,
but you are here with me.

Yes, you.

You are the best company
ever.

But let's not be foolish.

You exist at once
in all places
and times

and I am stuck
In this chair

and it is past time
for bed.

Fireworks, Hampton Beach, NH

Twice we endured
the exhilaration

of northern sky
ripped apart

the murder
of these lesser stars

twice leaving flushed
and murmuring

at once filled
and emptied

holding memory
against silence

bracing together
against the

now quiet
dark

The Piano Spilled Waltzes

Yes, dancing like magpies under stars,
Orion's belt dangling, you let down your hair.
My hands sought silken fire beyond auburn,
singing life gone madcap, forever and forever,
we twinkled liquid into black and white.

Always this Way

We say our prayers to hunger
and call them love

mostly on the wrong side of doors
tried and reluctantly forgotten

around and around we go
dark and light and repeat

I speak for myself
but most of us are framed
by desperate moments

someone saying they are cold
words written on guarded paper
the heart taking in what it can

everything ends before
your condition is cured

the hunger is never sated

The Day Requires Sacrifice but I am Not Its Martyr

I am content
to sit upon
this forgiving couch
and fiddle
with small dreams

while others
bleed and prosper

as light
sneaks through
the blinds
to dance upon
my dingy curtains
and beckon to my
shadowed walls

Unknown

I wish you
knew my name
dear one
my real name
the name
given by the gods
I wish you
could say it
and I could hear
I wish I could
tell you
your own

Always for Jill

The cat cradling herself
in my hand
tells me the story again
of how it was
when you and I
found each other
in the smoke and starlight
and you in my hands
was all the need
the world could endure

Once Upon

She unlocks the door, opens it.
He stands for a long moment.
His eyes take her in like water.
Do you wonder which way he is
expected to go?
More than a story hangs in the balance.
He moves. She lets him.
Memory persists.

Gone Dancing

After she left
I walked home
in the night

The forest
became
too
holy
for me
to stay

Hours later
I went back
to see
the moon
but the moon
had gone
dancing

I decided
to do
the same

The Apartment

A cup of MJB coffee
after half a bottle of pills
hard slaps to the face
and a shot of something
in the right arm
walking the floor for hours
the beautiful girl
in your bed
gin rummy and tears
and she still loves
the other one

The Woman Poet

The woman poet wears a thin black dress,
her breasts loose beneath, nipples dancing,
screaming look at me, hair in tight waves like
a medieval woodcut of a milkmaid or a nymph.

I picture her sweating, grunting, her strokes relieving
a cow's discomfort, or mine, or lying naked
in a forest, worshipful creatures gathered about her,
a lucky swan or bull nuzzling parted thighs.

She smiles, her eyes like crystal lightning, striking,
looking for the truest conductor,
hinting a feast you can almost taste.

I bet, too young to understand, she dreamt of sticky suckers
going liquid in her mouth, tongue swimming in warm saliva,
the dull ache of frustration, of wanting but not knowing what,
waking with tiny fingers still hiding
in the folds of an even-then-wise vagina.

I bet as she got older
boys took her into cars or down along riverbanks
and traded their awkward lust for her holy abandon
and believed, most of them, the conquest was theirs.

And now in a woman's body,
the girlish glow mixed with ripe curves
and fire and poetry, she glides into my fingertips,
whispering secrets and grinning, and slowly spins away.

The Problem with Words

You say "July" like it's a real month,
something you can hold
between your fingers or kiss
so I figure it's not quite as sloppy
as a persimmon
but close
and then there is rain
and everyone walking
with heads together
and speaking
in dramatic whispers
you say "August"
unaware I was born
in those hot days
so I guess it must be solid
like your hands on the steering wheel
and the baby we never made
asleep in the backseat
you say "goodbye for now"
and wander into the rainbow
while I think about a late lunch
in the first days of April
when the waitress promised us delights
that never came and watch you go
watch you go watch you go

A Certain Day in August

cracked glass
and a busy signal
on the telephone
stuck tires in loose earth
hair hanging in your eyes
the sun hot as death
sweat precious as blood
memories of fingers
dancing on your back
six beers by ten a.m.
all the candles burning
and that one face
that mattered
on a certain day
in August
when the world
still spun straight
or seemed to

Dancers

How they twirl
skirts billowing into
cotton clouds
of flowers and paisley
intricate, shifting patterns
repeat and vanish
never quite the same
all sex and gladness
stomp and glide
applause, applause
hugs and goodbye
the room itself alive
even later
in its own dark silence
the boards, the walls,
may yet remember

Jon and Gypsy

New Orleans in the '60s
French Quarter starving
and Gypsy sold her paintings
on the sidewalk
for bread and paper and ink.

Jon sweated blood and books,
he sweated miracles.
And the books appeared from
nowhere but Jon and Gypsy's
sweat and vision and determined,
hungry grace.

And she is past 100 and he is long dead.
And the books are in special rooms
in special libraries
or passed among collectors
for many dollars.

They gave us Bukowski and Miller,
The Outsider, hope, blinding, ragged joy,
days of glory and hope and hope and hope.

Did you know that Jon was a writer?
That he wrote a great prison novel?
That the two of them were arrested
one 1950s Christmas Eve, just for talking
to a black friend on a New Orleans street?

How can any story this rare be true?

Jon, Gypsy.
Jon, Gypsy.
Jon, Gypsy.

How you must delight the gods.
How they must smile at the thought of you.

In This Life

the blank inside old keys
locks misplaced
in the bright moon

we must allow ourselves
odd hats
and place signs
where they might be seen
by unknown family

sometimes the dance
is secret

like chipped pages
from obscure 1950s
magazines

things we barely notice
provide clues
but not everything fits

though it is hard to forget
the music of gone years

a face glimpsed once
in unlikely circumstance

or that pulpy
mildewed smell

But It's Okay

we were already dancing
when the night turned salt and vast
so no one stopped us
no one had the nerve
and our steps kept time
with the clock of desire
and you were light and shadow
in my arms
as the waiters stopped
to watch and clap
and the old man in the corner
the Lithuanian captain
from a hundred forgotten wars
laughed and cavorted
like a youth enthralled
by coy chance

we were already dancing
and it was clear we would not stop
even as the last notes
from the last song
the last great music
of the world
tinkled silent
and night left
and everything disappeared
slowly then all at once
and I was alone and dancing
and you would return
I was sure of it

but of course
I was wrong
and the dance and I
like fools
we persisted
even until this moment
even until now

Like You, I Cannot Breathe

Old letters lost in the mail
unconsidered secret lives
flowers left unwatered
and dried to paper bone

False smiles
of ancient strangers
only you can see

Photos of dubious origin
leading to unfinished highways

The meaning beneath the flow

Somewhere there is a person
who knows the intent
of light

But they are lost
in the air
forcing the world
to remain a riddle
too small to carry

Like you I have questions
I cannot quite pose
and the answers
are all drowned

Drenched

In the rain the flowers bursting
in the ghost rain
in the rain bleeding strangers
in the hot rain unforgiven of my sins
in the hot driving rain hard as rocks
in the rain that would kill us if it could
in the rain where I won't see you again
in the rain invisible
in the ghost rain
in the rain the flowers bursting

Please Be Quiet

Screaming lets them
take you away.
It lets them take you
to a place
where screaming
makes sense.
Where someone
might say
they'll give you
something
to scream about
and then do it.
It shows them
who you are
when everything
is pounded
to dust.

Sue Me

The beautiful girl
wearing a tasteful,
grey pleated skirt
white cardigan
matching knee socks
black rimmed glasses
and riding her bicycle
across campus
crashed
legs akimbo
on the sidewalk
in front of my car
providing a startling view
of her remarkable legs
almost to, I assume,
her panties
(color unknown)
and though I felt
true compassion
for her plight
(much, I imagine,
in the way of the Buddha)
I did not burden myself
with guilt
for looking

Trying To Tell You Something

In the way professors love
in the way of spiders
in the way of forgotten bones
hidden in old attics
even brave children avoid
in the way of dust
in the way of books
propped up by dullards
and their pride
in the way of wind
blowing everything clean
and water drowning what
tries to be alive
in the way of going home
to find nothing there
but what remains
of nothing

Bouquet (*for Kate Bloom*)

On the Chattanooga streets
hungry of course and beautiful
against all odds
a dwindling perk of youth
the chance at porn
pulled her head above
one certain death
into another
and in a book-lined room
sitting for an interview
with a man who
makes it his business
to question girls like her
she answers that eating
is one of her favorite things
and with feral snap
and eyes that know more
than they ever should
that steak is her
favorite food

Search her name
on the Internet
and you will find her
pleasing the desperate
still too thin
living the only
available glamour
in nice clothes
when dressed

In ten years she sees
herself married
rich and happy
a better job
worked into a better
place in life
and she can still laugh
even smile
though ten years
is a long time
too long
not long enough

Strange Actress

Some say unhinged
in their unkind way.

Mostly she is an extra.

No lines to past or future
or even to the coffee shop
around the corner
where awkward conversation
costs more than she makes
in a week.

You might say she's stuck.

The lines go on in her head
where everything
is close up, Mr. DeMille.

Some say crazy

but she knows
they can't see her.

That's the beauty of dying
while everything's still wet
with anticipation.

Someone needs to tell her
it's time for places, please.

Action.
Cut.

That's a wrap.

Portable Life

Be unkind and call her noise.
Is that enough?

She has no defense
against apathy.

Be unkind and measure her
against comfort.

That's what people do.

Even the streets don't care
to learn her name.

Be unkind.
That is your way.

Be the one who closes the final door.

She was once beautiful
but the parched road
took even that.

Be unkind and call her nothing.
Her face tells every story.

Failure to Communicate

you wonder that
far flung worlds
do not speak to us
and decide they
are void
while they
on those worlds
wonder
that we do not
understand
how to listen
that we do not see
everything
is dance
that they
are blowing kisses
to the stars

Perspective

There are worlds beyond knowing
worlds you can't get to from here
because their direction makes no sense
in this place we live

there are worlds so grand and subtle
you could not see them
even if you were swimming inside
(and you probably are
right this second)

and in an infinite number of these worlds
(which still is only a small fraction
of their number)
there are creatures who wonder
if worlds other than their own exist
who wonder what might live there
who wonder, my friend, about you

these creatures would give most anything
to know your mind
to see your face

they would sacrifice everything
to understand your intimate desires
or even share a cup of coffee
(they like coffee everywhere)

there are worlds beyond these
so far beyond these worlds
that they do not even wonder

we call these worlds by nameless names
and they are more real
than you could hope to be

you, my friend, are a hot shadow
in the darkest corner of heaven

all things considered
and from the larger perspective
not a pretty place to be

It's Simple

Casablanca
is Ilsa's story
told through
Rick's eyes

so the truth
about her love
can't be
pinned down

that's why
it's magic

Faulkner
used the same trick
with Caddy
and her brothers

with the same result

and here's
another thing:

in the end,
it's best to be Lazlo

There was a Time

lost days
and the rustle of dry leaves
ancient boards holding
what remains of history
beneath skies that look
like skies have always looked
and air that feels
like air has always felt
on our skin and in our lungs
this music plays
as a question to time
and an answer that moves
an inch past our fingers
and into the mirror of the spirits
where everything is dance
oh, lost
oh, lost
I hear you now
and you have all my tears
all my promises

Just So

Everything
shows in
the way
you hold
the child's
hand

like a
years-long
time lapse
photograph

from so tight
they cannot
get away
to firm enough
for them
to notice

but not
so hard
as to make
them believe
they are
caught

High Dive

hard smack
onto concrete
edge everything
quick and still
I couldn't taste
the blood didn't
know my palate
was broken   a
lady gave the
lifeguard a yellow
tissue   carried
eight years old
to my parents
nobody panicked
had me back in
the water by
august

The Cat

In China they have strippers
at funerals
but my cat doesn't care.

She has snuck into the backyard
to listen to the birds sing

and to sniff at the hair I cut
from my head
and tossed out
so the birds might use it
for their nests.

Orson Welles
once fought Ernest Hemingway
in a movie projection booth
but my cat doesn't care.

She sits on the patio
bathed in birdsong
while the birds ignore the hair
I left for them
and the Chinese crack down
on the funeral strippers.

I think we can agree
Orson Welles
was damned lucky
Papa didn't bust him up
and the Chinese know how
to send a man to the next world

as my cat creeps back inside
and the birds stop singing
and the dog, so above it all,
lies sleeping beside me on the couch.

The cat doesn't care.

Chicken Fiasco

The chicken needs work.
It is mostly bones
with bits of muscle attached
in strategic places
like near the wings and anus.
The chicken is angry
and who could blame it?
Who would want to be
in this condition?
No one I know.
The chicken came in
for a regular session
and something went wrong. Horribly.
Now the chicken
is pretty much disassembled.
It will have a terrible time getting home.
Just making it back to the bus stop
seems impossible.
In the village, everyone
is preparing for the party.
The chicken is the guest of honor
and probably won't even show up.
The chicken should fucking sue,
if you ask me.
Even when it finally trudges home,
it will still be without its feathers.
Little Mary, the chicken's tiny friend,
will weep for days.

Bad Night on the Town

The chicken hated that her date smoked. Allergies.
She would have a migraine later for certain.
But the night was young and who knew when
she was going to end up with a wrung neck,
slowly digesting as somebody's dinner?
Blind dates were the worst. God, yes.
She had never understood that until just this second.

Hot Hot Hot

I am burning like a rat in the desert
burning like a seed in the mind of Zeus
burning like the octopus
lost in dark currents
burning like the player
who becomes the ball
burning like the flame of lonely nights
bent over blank pages
burning like stars laced with bourbon
burning like the plain girl
finding courage
to cut in
at the final dance of summer
burning like the tears of the old
I am the fire of every chance
wasted or giving light
and I am burning like the dreams
you hold in silence
this moment and forever
in your secret and famished
vicious
tender heart

Six Pack

I.
I didn't say "kowtow."
I said "cow towel"
like on the farm
after a rain.

II.
Some dogs never have their day,
you insensitive bastard.
The possums see to it.

III.
Clop clop clop clop clop clop clop.

IV.
Did you SEE that?
Did YOU see that?
Did you see THAT?

V.
Hand me a coconut. I believe they's rats.

VI.
The clouds parted and the cows went dancing.
That's how the world works, bub.

Pees

Poems are made
by fools like me

But Donald Trump
drinks hooker pee

Some Kind of Patriotic Trip

It is important the child be astonished.
Broken shells washed up by waves.
Sometimes whole, but never the longed for conch.
The fireworks started last night
and no one noticed but her mother and I
watching by the pool.
Darkness interrupted by flash and sparkle.
Small kabooms in the air.

The Gulf is a warm welcome
once you get your shoulders wet.
Sophie worries only a little
about what might be
swimming around our legs.
I worry about what we don't
know how to consider.
We laugh and talk and splash around.

Today we'll buy our rockets.
Everything will explode over the water.
The children and their desperate parents
will gaze at rote celebration
staccato between the Gulf and the sky.
Orion is up there to find, we all think we know.
Down here on earth, sparklers will have to do
for the smallest hands.
Astonished is too big to hope for
but we hope anyway.

You Know the Ones I Mean

The great and boring dead
and the children they murder
through endless days chained to desks
and presumptuous in their weighty books
the ashes of forever
with meanings to be picked over
like the bones of a mackerel
on an old lady's blue plate special
at a diner that should have closed
ten years back
the dead who had something to say
and said it in the manner
the professors enjoy
the dead still getting revenge
on the innocent
while cats stare into the wind
dogs chase bones
the tides continue to rise
and the children pray in vain
for the afternoon bell to save them

It's Probably Just Me

How many
times a day
do I say,
usually under
my breath,
"God! What is wrong
with you people?"
And, while I have
my theories,
the answer,
ultimately,
remains
unclear.

The End of Things

Time cracked open
and God spilled out
the infinite unknowable egg
shattered

God
shy as a poor girl
in a thrift store dress
on the first day of kindergarten
and afraid to speak
to her beautiful classmates
spilled out

and not built for this world
died quickly from exposure

everything vanished
leaving not so much
as starless space
or a green
plastic Buddha
the kind an artistic child
might desire
but be denied
by her dull parents
on holiday
as a cheap
and holy
souvenir

How It Goes with Some

Some go lost in the woods
with backpacks
filled with last effects and stars
the living witness
to whatever might happen
in the secret going
some go mad
in front of television screens
or while drinking coffee
in trendy restaurants or, better,
in greasy dives
of unremarkable small towns
nowhere near any other place
some go racing through streets
lit by neon promises
that never come true
some disappear into bottles
or the pages of books
that will go unread forever
some go up in acetylene glory
and some dissolve on couches
in living rooms like your own
and everything is hard
until it is over
but eventually
everything is

Lost

Photographs in the morning
of Sara Murphy and Duff Twysden
and someone's memories
of laughing in French Cafes
long ago. Pictures of Picasso
and Fitzgerald and Gerald Murphy.
Hemingway, of course.

Old stories told to death.
Threads in a blue sweater
unraveled and stored away.
Champagne, ladies. Champagne.
Memories belong to everyone now.
Sara Murphy with her frizzy hair.
Endless romance out of reach.

The Poets

The poets die if we let them
and the stars blink out
the maidens grow old
the world cracks open
and nothing is forever
not even time
and the poets
prefer to bleed
but fade if we let them
and the birds fly south
and children become things
we cannot imagine
and the poets
tell the fortunes of man
while dying a little
each day
alone in small rooms
with nothing but angels
and none of them
have wings
but they fly
just the same
while the poets
bear witness
to the coming dark
and no one
gives a damn

When We Scream

We who dance
dance

And we who sing
sing

And we who carry your burdens
also carry our own

When we play
we bleed
when we scream
we live
when we fight
we laugh

and when we kill the unkind light
we wait in the smothering darkness
for you

Here is Truth for You

Hate on
Bukowski

or ignore him
you enlightened

but he wrote
as he pleased

and is
remembered.

This is enough
for anyone

and more
probably

than will ever
be said of you.

At the Feet of the Master

If you think
Bukowski's
greatness
lies in his writing
about sex
his drunkenness
and his cursing
you do not
understand
Bukowski
nor do you
understand
what it means
to be great

Motion Sickness

The sutras confirmed what you already understood:

All life is suffering.

And your message was clear, but clearly misunderstood as they took to the highways in search of your ghost with you still breathing.

Explication

I want poems hard as coal
not diamond hard but coal hard

coal flakes and smears
within a basic integrity

diamond stays diamond—

the facets remain sharp and cold
and may cut you—

but the sparkle doesn't rub off

see?

coal sustains
coal makes you dirty

and holds fire within itself
and wants to burn

needs only a nudge into flame
from paper and match

your match

coal fire
coal poem

hard and black and burning

I Love My Readers

I do not
remember
what I wrote
on that
bathroom wall,
only how pleased
I was
when an
acquaintance
came back
into the classroom
after our break
laughing about
the wonderful thing
he had found written
there
words I agreed
were brilliant
but never
acknowledged
as my own
until now.

Original

In its original form the word
was light, the train
a flash across
the prairie. The dog
a hiccup of love.
In its original form the joke
was loving, the glass
on the shelf a promise
of touch, the original
form of starlight,
the original form
of loss, the original form
of remaining when
loved ones go.
In its original form
the wound told stories
and people
sometimes listened.
The original hope.

Legacy

Evidence of ancient poets
found in wind whipping waves
of Atlantic squall
in a particular handful
of Sahara sand
a thousand miles
from nowhere
lost epics and heroes
from forgotten minds
as real as blood stained shields
or the shadow of giant redwoods
unknown for ages
as necessary as air
or the bones in no one's grave

Wake the Fuck Up

Inside the dream
the dreamer dreams
inside the dreamer
dreams the dream
inside the dream

Coming Soon

Often the snakes
waltz three-quarter time
with the nails
holding me phallus-like
on this beloved candy cane
toot toot sez the daddy snake
wrapping around my legs
and up toward Mary
but my hands won't work
hanging here like a carp
I take my name in vain

Meaningful Dialog

Dying
       wit   less and
poor   doesn't
       matter
(fuck you fuckers you fu)
bet
       ter
men h
a
ve
faced
       oblivion with
less, as
my monkey   (ck you I said you cant sto)
       brain screams curses at the death in life
in me and in th   e world and my
potato hands
       grab fists
of whitene
ss as my marshmallow eyes spill
                     and burn
(p me u kant sht me up u freakin)
rivulets
    of fire
                     down sandpaper
       cheeks.
There ar
e no
answers and the trick is
never look past the smiling surfa (bastards I no

my rites I reed)   ce:
            beyond
lie only insensate
w
asps   hungr
        y
for your touch.
Forget the
            (things, I see things)   lily
            and the rose, keeping only the
                        thorns
as
            a
remin
der
                                    of
ultimate   reality.

And try not to
stumble, much, at least where
                they might see you:
the laughter stings worse
(Do you understand me, sir?)
            worse than the fall.
Cease
being
                brave when your time comes.
We have had enough false bravado and plain foolishness
from our
                        great   men

to last all
the ages.
(I sad, d'ya und)
better to le
t the madness
                        flow
            on your last breath
better

                ,

            better to end
with hon
            (erstand me, hashole? I kno things I)
est agony than try fooling God or your neighbor or yourself
(understand things I)
(see)   (you)   (right)
     but for now (now)
this is enough, and we do not see:
to sit
         alone
                    on a familiar stool sipping a beer
daintily, even, if that helps get you through
pushing back freight train
certainty with quiet calm on the outsideknowingthe luna
ticinyourchestandarmsand (promise me) eyes and mouth
can, will, come calling in his own good time.
this is enough
        (promise)
to understand the wasted hours
and, finally, forgive yourself the cost.

(It's very difficult you know you understand
            don't you you've
been there I no u'v been ther and
            why cant you taste the
                    blood
why
cnt u tase th blud
now)?

No Rest or Peace of Solitude

I wanted to laugh when the old man asked
"Are there any butterflies in your head
worth remembering?" The old coot standing there
like a totem pole and grinning at my discomfort
and I finally screaming

>   LEAVE ME
>   ALONE
>   YOU FREAKING
>   LOON!

I wanted to laugh but found that rock in my hand
and a skull is really very like an egg shell.

"Are there any butterflies are there any swallows,"
he sputtered as I put the quietus on *that* game.

Okay, I giggled, a little, licking my fingers
and pondered the same old tune:

The nuts, oh the nuts everywhere,
how do they find me?

Try This

Knock down a wall
and see what happens.
Things may collapse
or things may come through.

Maybe these will be awful things
or maybe light.

Dig a hole in your neighbor's yard
and watch what he does.
It won't be pretty.
But dig the hole deep,
if you're going to do it.

Dig your hole
so the neighbor knows
you meant it.

Dig it so he wonders why,
so he worries about the nut
who lives next door.

Knock down a man in the street.
Steal his comb or eyeglasses.
Touch his hair for luck.

Butcher random animals
in your basement
and present their bones to strangers
at social gatherings
to which you were not invited.

Walk naked through the storm.
Go with courage through broken walls.
Live everything in dreams.

Pax Americana

someday we will be the beggars
and we will send our young
in desperation
to those with plenty

and we will trust
in the goodness of their souls
because we will have no choice

and, oh, how we will lament
and cry and rend our clothing
when the children are spat upon
sacrificed
caged
or sent back
to the hell we have made

and we will become hatred
and we will become fury
and we will become revenge
for our children's sake

and terrible will be our wrath
and no one will care
except to mock us

mark it down

Rome is burning
and you'd best enjoy the show
while you can

Psychopathic White Cowards in Dumbass America Today

children in cages
white people
chanting hate

people who do not want others
to have food or shelter or medicine

bridges crumbling
poison water
policemen free to murder

little men with guns
demanding to see
your papers

the poor getting poorer
and caged by circumstance
while the rich are free
to walk the streets
as they please

blood will come of this
blood will stain the shining surfaces

children stolen from parents
white people afraid of everything

white people like a plague

white people looking for a leader
who hates who they hate
and finding him

children in cages
and white people
free to chant hate
free to chant hate
free to chant hate

America, just look
what you have done

it is almost too late for you, America

psychopathic country
a chanting white cult

children in cages
in our America

blood will come of this
blood will drown us all

Bad Day

I'm having a bad day
in my nice house.

I'm having a bad day
with my two cars
and plenty of food
on my shelves.

I'm having a bad day
with my clean clothing
my advanced degrees
and my good job.

I'm having a bad day
with my white skin
and my plenty.

I'm having a bad day
even with every advantage.

I'm having a bad day
even with the world tilted hard
in my favor.

Can you believe it?

It's hard, I know.

Now, think of all the people
who have none of these things

and think of the bad day
they might be having.

Think of the empty shelves.
Think of having to walk two miles
to buy a gallon of milk
and walk back home
with its weight.

Think of that being you

or wondering where
you will live next week
when the rent money is gone.

Think of children without hope.

Think of necessary medicine
out of reach.

Think of being hated for
how you look
who you love
or where, by pure chance,
you were born.

I'm having a bad day
in my nice house

and I know I am unimaginably lucky.

I know there is a chance
I will feel better tomorrow
and all my nice things
will still be here.

Isn't that swell?
Aren't you pleased for me?
Yes?
Yes?

And how are you
wherever you might be?

How is your day?

I truly want to know.

Get Your Peanuts

The circus leaves rings
in dirt and greasepaint
smeared across
an abandoned lot
a creaking calliope
unknown to children
grown old
who forget themselves
with arthritic shoulders
trick knees
bad vision even at noon
as clowns pile up
with holes in their backs
smoldering
come one come all
the lions are hungry

Dead Man's Hand

I'm aces and eights
and the world
is a spike in my neck
while the girls dance
in red satin

Their legs shine
in the dirty boys' eyes
and make the hog washer's
day bearable

I'm the spent shell in the street
the empty chamber
the stranger swinging from a rope

While love goes
for five dollars
in the upstairs rooms

I'm the body in the alley
and the half-finished bottle

Cover me in sheets and cry
if you like
but place your bets

Let's settle this sorry business
and get on down to Hell

This is So

Every day
when I feel
like dying
I breathe
instead

not focused
yoga breath
or inhaling
golden energy
or being the light

I breathe like a man
caught in a web
and watching hard
as the spiders
edge closer

a man who has
to work a job
who has children
to feed

a man shattered
like a dropped glass

every day
when I feel
like dying
I stifle screams
and stare
straight ahead

breathing in
breathing out

and when I see
those who know
my name
I smile and wave
and maybe
we exchange
pleasant words
or even embrace

while the spiders
arrive
to love me
like only
spiders can

everywhere

every day
every day
every day

breathing in
breathing out

when I feel like this
caught in a web
when I feel like dying

Grateful acknowledgment is made to the following, where some of these poems have been accepted or previously appeared, sometimes in slightly different form.

Alien Buddha Press, Alien Buddha Zine, Appalachian Heritage, Betray the Invisible, Chiron Review, Gypsy Art Show, Hemispheres, Inscape, Masks are Never Enough, Pink Cadillac, Poetry Feast, Protea Poetry Journal, Pressure Press Presents, Rust Belt Press, Rust Belt Review, 3 Quarks Daily, Winedrunk Sidewalk, Wingnut Brigade.

Jeff Weddle grew up in Prestonsburg, a small town in the hill country of eastern Kentucky. He has worked as a public library director, disc jockey, newspaper reporter, Tae Kwon Do teacher, and fry cook, among other things. His first book, *Bohemian New Orleans: The Story of the Outsider and Loujon Press* (University Press of Mississippi, 2007), won the Eudora Welty Prize and helped inspire Wayne Ewing's documentary, *The Outsiders of New Orleans: Loujon Press* (Wayne Ewing Films, 2007). He teaches in the School of Library and Information Studies at the University of Alabama.

colophon

Dead Man's Hand, by Jeff Weddle,
was set with Trebuchet MS fonts
by SpiNDec, Port Saint Lucie, Florida
The jacket and covers were designed by
Kris Haggblom, Port Saint Lucie, Florida

www.ingramcontent.com/pod-product-compliance
Lightning Source LLC
Chambersburg PA
CBHW030059100526
44591CB00008B/205